THOUGHT CATALOG BOOKS

Does This Bible Belt Make Me Look Gay?

Does This Bible Belt Make Me Look Gay?

KRISTA DOYLE

Thought Catalog Books

Brooklyn, NY

THOUGHT CATALOG BOOKS

 Published by Thought Catalog Books, a division of The Thought & Expression Co., Williamsburg, Brooklyn. Founded in 2010, Thought Catalog is a website and imprint dedicated to your ideas and stories. We publish fiction and non-fiction from emerging and established writers across all genres. For general information and submissions: manuscripts@thoughtcatalog.com.

First print edition, 2016

ISBN 978-1533496331

10 9 8 7 6 5 4 3 2 1

Cover design by © KJ Parish

Contents

Introduction

Hello, dear reader, and welcome to my book! I'm not really sure what information I'm supposed to divulge about said book in this introduction. I suppose I'll just go ahead and let you know that if you've come here expecting to find me standing proud and steadfast on a soapbox, you will not find that. If you've come expecting me to break down Biblical theology in order to sway your political leanings one way or another, you will not find that. I will be sparing you all from my political opinions because pretty much the only thing I know about politics is that President Obama knows Beyoncé and he sometimes comes to Los Angeles to ruin my work commute. So, no, we won't be talking politics. There are smarter, better people out there writing those types of books.

This book is simply a collection of stories about my experiences as someone who came from both sides of this cultural coin, my experiences as a lesbian raised as a Christian in the South. These stories contain the people and places that made me who I am today. They contain all the horrible mistakes I've made and all the embarrassing moments I thought I'd never live through. They probably contain the word "journey" an annoying amount of times, but that is what these stories are to me—my journey.

I hope that you'll be able to laugh with me (or at me) as you read about how I gracelessly and awkwardly stumbled my way into becoming the semi-functioning human I am today. I hope that you'll be able to learn from my mistakes in case you should ever find yourself in similar situations. I hope that the sticky mess that was my path to self-discovery will help you through your own.

1

For As Long As I Can Remember: Christianity vs. Homosexuality

Christianity

I got saved when I was 7. "Getting saved" in the world of the Southern Baptist means that you've accepted Jesus as your Lord and Savior. At the age of 7, what did that even mean to me? For starters, I knew it meant that I wouldn't be going to hell. I didn't really understand what hell was, but I knew it involved fire and pain and weird creatures and probably Josh Johnson from 3rd period math who always told me I needed braces. And why wasn't I more afraid of pledging my allegiance to a man who referred to himself using the term "Lord and Savior"? Sure, pal, I've never seen you, and I don't know much about you, but by all means, take Lordship over my life. I knew that Jesus was a guy we always talked about who probably smelled like mud and was sort of like Santa in that he was always watching me, but was definitely not as useful as Santa because he had never given me a bicycle or a Barbie doll or even one of those stocking stuffer candy canes filled with red and green M&Ms. Jesus was my all-powerful Lord and

Savior, but couldn't even give me candy at Christmas? I let it slide because, apparently, Jesus was the difference between me spending eternity in heaven with all the other saved people or in hell talking about my crooked teeth with Josh Johnson.

So, it was decided. I had to stay on Jesus' good side. I figured I had a pretty good shot at this considering church was basically my whole life. I grew up in a small (reeeally small), Southern (reeeally Southern) town where every Sunday morning, Sunday night, and Wednesday night, I took my spot on the church pew to listen to my Grandpa preach from the stage. I went to Sunday School and colored pictures of Bible characters while my Grandma told us their stories and the lessons we should learn from them. I sang along to hymns as my mom led the choir from the church piano. I learned all about Jesus and Satan, angels and demons, the Garden of Eden and the Lake of Fire. I went to Bible studies and church retreats. I was taught that everything was black and white, that there was a well-defined line between right and wrong and, as Christians, we were never to cross that line.

Church felt like a part of me growing up. It was this thing I did because my family did it and because it made me feel good about myself and because we always got to eat fried chicken at my grandparents' house afterwards. It was like an old habit that I didn't understand, but knew I should do anyway. Even at 7, I had a lot of questions about the things I was learning. A lot of the concepts and rules confused me and I didn't understand why certain things and people were viewed as terrible and "sinful," but I decided that if staying on Jesus' good side meant thinking these things, then I would just have to think them, too.

Homosexuality

The year is 1992. The season is Christmas. The TV channel is VH1. I'm 5 years old and watching Bon Jovi's *Please Come Home For Christmas* music video, which also starred supermodel Cindy Crawford. This is my first memory of being attracted to another woman. It wasn't a sexual attraction or anything (though CC does know her way around the tiny denim cut-offs she's sporting in said video), but I do remember being drawn to her in a way that I hadn't experienced before. I wanted to hug her and be close to her and smell her hair. These experiences would continue to happen as I got older, as I began to find myself more and more emotionally and physically drawn to women, not men. I remember watching Disney movies and not wishing to be the princess, but wishing to be the one storming the castles and fighting the dragons, wishing to be the one who gets to rescue the damsel in distress.

As I got older, the feelings continued and I became a little more aware of the fact that not all girls felt these things. I harbored a nerdy freshman crush on the captain of the cheerleading squad while trying to teach myself to like it when I kissed a boy. I had to like kissing boys because that's what I was supposed to like, right? If there was one thing I had learned from countless church services, Bible studies, and summer church retreats, it was that Christianity did not smile upon those with homosexual thoughts. In fact, a lot of the Christians I was around at the time, hated homosexuality and would often isolate and look down on any gay person who dared cross their path. So, I convinced myself that my thoughts about girls meant nothing and that they would go away with time, or when I met that "special guy." I pushed my thoughts down into the deep, dark recesses of my mind where things go to never be thought of again, things like bad haircuts and that time in the 4th grade when my teacher caught me sending myself a love note because I wanted to be like Cher from *Clueless*.

I went through high school and college an emotional mess, constantly trying to be something I wasn't. On the outside, a shiny, happy Christian who went to youth group and abstinence club meetings and wore T-shirts with Bible puns on them. I did my best to live up to the t-shirts, but on the inside, I was an angry, bitter, confused, scared girl who thought that God had just made her incorrectly, like one of those cans of beans at the grocery store that you can get for half-off because it was bent when it came from the factory. I was the "bent can of beans" of Christianity. I would listen to my friends gush about their boyfriends, then go home and ask God why he didn't make me "normal" like them. I would ask why he would give me the capacity to be attracted to and develop real feelings for someone he didn't want me to be with. I would pray to meet a guy that I liked so I didn't have to feel this way anymore. I was completely immersed in a faith that promised freedom and peace and was miserable.

For as long as I can remember, these were the two worlds I was caught between. The majority of my life has been spent battling who I really am vs. who I thought I needed to be. So many times I felt like a kid caught in the middle of a messy divorce, being made to pick a side. If I picked Christianity, I would be culturally accepted in my small Louisiana town, but I would eventually have to, gulp, marry a man, lest I be deemed an old maid, which would then (surprise, surprise) land me back outside the area of cultural acceptance. If I chose homosexuality, I would no doubt be a bit of an outcast. People may be nice to my face, but would be saving all their insults and righteous opinions for behind my back. That was the Southern way, after all. It was quite the dilemma to have, for as long as I can remember.

2

The 10 Most Southern Things I've Ever Done

People always get so curious about my upbringing when I tell them that I'm from Louisiana: Was your house on a swamp? Have you ever done voodoo? Will you cook me some gumbo? The answers to those questions are, respectively: No, no, and I wish I knew how. Even still, my childhood was very Southern. I fished in creeks. People I knew wore cowboy hats non-ironically. Boys would get excused from school because it was the first day of deer hunting season. When I say I grew up in the South, I mean my town could not have gotten anymore Southier than it was. To help give the curious minds a better idea of just how Southern of an upbringing I had, I have compiled a list of the top ten most Southern things I've done over the years. Some of this might be illegal, I'm still not sure.

1. Drove over an hour to the next town carrying a small alligator in a bucket in the backseat of my car. I may or may not have been (but definitely was) delivering it to someone so they could make fried alligator legs at a later date. Its tail kept flopping over the side of the bucket and I was sure I was going to die.

2. Helped my brother raise flying squirrels. We brought them places with us on tiny leashes made of shoelaces and he would sell them to his friends. They almost never bit us.

3. Rode in the bucket of my Paw Paw's tractor on a regular basis.

4. Had pet raccoons. And a pet deer. And a pet cat who killed my pet deer (RIP).

5. Drove my stepdad's giant diesel engine Ford F350 truck with a lift kit to school every day. I was 16 and could barely see over the steering wheel.

6. Had my Sweet 16th birthday party in my grandparents' cow pasture. We had a bonfire and sat on the back of pickup trucks and hay bales. The cows were also in attendance.

7. Helped my Paw Paw mix "slop" (food) to feed his pigs.

8. Played in a barn on a regular basis. Yes, it had a tire swing. And hay. And baby chickens.

9. Helped my dad skin squirrels he killed while hunting so we could use the meat in our gumbo.

10. Chased rogue cows down the street on my bike trying to get them back into their appropriate, cow safety-approved areas.

Please inquire privately for numbers 11-100.

3

Kissing All the Frogs

1. Charlie

Charlie was my first boyfriend. It's an age-old story, really. I was lining up for recess when one of Charlie's friends came up to me in all his 4th grade glory. "Hey," he said, in a tone of voice that clearly implied I had just won the lottery of lotteries since he was speaking to me. "Charlie said he wants to go out with you. Will you go out with him?" I didn't know what he meant by the term "going out," as we were 10, and the only people I hung out with outside of school were characters from NBC's "Must See TV" line-up. Even still, I said yes, because Charlie was a hot commodity at my elementary school and I was no fool. Charlie smiled and waved at me from across the room and I waved back, igniting the flame that was our romance. Three months passed and Charlie and I were going strong. Notes were passed. Giggly "hellos" were exchanged in the hallways. Glances were stolen on the playground from the safety of our respective friend groups. We were pretty hot and heavy, until one day in 5th period English, when it all came crashing down.

"Guess what I heard," whispered my friend, Kelly. "Charlie kissed a girl named Haley at the skating rink Friday night." Um, excuse me? I was outraged. Partly because Charlie had betrayed our sacred bond and partly because my mom NEVER allowed me to go to the skating rink on weekend nights. The skating rink was my favorite place, but I was only allowed to go on Saturday afternoons when someone had a birthday party because the middle school kids would go on weekend nights to make out during couples' skate. "I don't want to kiss, I just want to blade!" I would try to explain, but there was no use. "He cheated on me?" I thought to myself. "I'll bet it's because I wanted to skate to Kenny Loggins songs at Brooke's birthday party last weekend." No, I could not, would not blame this on Kenny Loggins. The full blame landed on Charlie and we parted ways that day.

A few years later, Charlie re-entered the scene. We were in 7th grade now, both older, wiser. I was 13 and everybody I knew had already had their first kiss, except me. I kept telling myself that I wanted to wait for someone special, but I grew tired of being left out and decided that Charlie would have to do. We kissed one day in front of my Gateway computer screen while playing Oregon Trail. My friend Katelyn was there to make sure my mom didn't catch us. It was quite romantic. After we kissed, I turned to Katelyn, said, "Please go get me a glass of water," and kept hunting for buffalo to feed the weary travelers in my wagon party. The next day at school he told everyone I was a bad kisser and I told everyone that he died of dysentery before we could even make it to Fort Kearny.

2. Parker

Parker came along around the time that the word "boyfriend" was starting to mean a little more than passing each other love notes on your way from 3rd period science to 4th period math, which was unfortunate for him because it was also about the same time I realized it didn't come naturally to me to want the things that came with the new, upgraded version of the word "boyfriend." But, I was supposed to have a boyfriend because all my friends had boyfriends and I definitely didn't want them thinking I was as weird as I felt. Parker and I fought a lot because he said I never wanted to hang out with him as much as my friends wanted to hang out with their boyfriends. He even asked me once if I was secretly gay, saying that he didn't like how much I talked about Maureen, an upperclassmen who was dating his best friend. 15-year-old Krista was, of course, appalled when he asked that question and I strongly denied his accusations even though I knew he had a point. He broke up with me a few weeks later in front of the football team before a pep rally and I decided I shouldn't talk about Maureen anymore.

3. Stephen

"But I don't want to kiss him," I whispered to my best friend Kelly. We were standing in my kitchen and her boyfriend was outside listening to music in his car, as was his friend Stephen. Kelly and I were inseparable, but so were her and her boyfriend, so there was often some poor unfortunate soul dragged along with us in hopes I would hit it off with him and would no longer be the third wheel. "Oh, just do it. Just have fun for once," she retorted. I kissed a lot of guys in high school because I felt like I had to. Stephen was one of them.

We went back outside to meet the boys at the car and I

decided to try and give Stephen a chance. I listened for what felt like 137 years to him talking about baseball, hunting, and how he still hadn't read "that crap" for Mrs. Harrison's English class (and by "that crap." he meant The Great Gatsby). We kissed for a little while at the end of the night. He used too much tongue and I thought about how I never again wanted to kiss someone who hated The Great Gatsby.

4. Michael

Michael was my date to Junior Prom. He was a friend of a friend who went to school one town over from ours. Apparently, I caught his eye one evening outside of our local Burger Inn, which must have been during a rare moment when I wasn't double fisting cheeseburgers into my mouth. Before we got to prom, I overheard him telling our mutual friend that he was going to try and touch my boobs at the after party. No thanks, good sir. To discourage his mission, I spent the whole night at the refreshments table talking to my teachers instead of out on the dance floor. Eventually, he left to go find other, more accessible chests and I got a ride with friends to the after party where the only thing to touch my boobs was a little bit of chili that dropped from my hot dog.

5. Matt

Matt and I broke up during my senior year of college. It was my favorite breakup of any breakup I've ever had or ever will have. He invited me to lunch at my favorite local cafe, McDonald's. After debating what delicious garbage we were going to put into our bodies, we sat down with our nuggets and fries and got down to business. "You see," he said, picking up a chicken nugget. "Right now, to me, girls are like chicken nuggets." If he didn't have my attention before, he had it now. Was I offended or was I intrigued? Intrigued, I decided. "Go on…" I thought to myself.

"Usually, chicken nuggets are good. They're the greatest! But you know how sometimes you eat too many nuggets? And then you feel sick, like you're going to throw up? That's kind of how I feel. Right now, it's like, if I have to eat ONE more chicken nugget…" he looked at the nugget he was holding for a minute before taking a bite. "You know?" he asked, mouth full of nug. Strangely, I did know. I couldn't even be offended or mad at him. Plus, we had already been dating for two whole weeks, so I was looking for an out anyway.

Without realizing it, Matt had just put into words (ridiculous words, but words nonetheless) my entire outlook on dating. That nugget metaphor stayed with me, and I thought of it often as I continued trying to date guys during college. "If I have to eat ONE more chicken nugget…" I would often joke with myself after I lost interest in yet another date. Luckily, Matt and I are still friends and he'll always be my favorite ex-boyfriend. He eventually found and married the chicken nugget that will never make him sick and I secretly credit him for helping me realize I just wasn't 'bout that nug life.

6. David

David was the last boyfriend I had. It was the summer after I graduated college, and we were both working at a Christian summer camp in New Orleans. I was a camp counselor to 30 horribly-behaved 5th graders who taught me about Nicki Minaj while I taught them about Noah's Ark and David was a dreamy guitar player in the camp worship band who sang hymns while all of the preteens swooned. David and I had a strange relationship, to say the least. Our activity of choice was marathoning *Lost,* Season 1 on his couch. Sometimes we would hold hands. I found it strange, but comforting, that he never wanted to kiss or touch me. We got along great, but there was an obvious lack of spark for both of us and I was okay with that. I had someone to hang out with, which would keep my question-asking family at bay, but I didn't have to worry about trying to find new ways to avoid the physical aspect of a relationship.

I didn't have to avoid the physical aspect, because David did most of that for me. This was most apparent one day when David and I took a day-trip to the beach. We were playing in the waves, when I got smacked pretty hard. I tumbled around underwater a bit and when I came up, I heard a loud gasp as I wiped the water from my eyes. I opened them up to see David covering his with both of his hands. My top had come off during my underwater adventure and my boobs were on display for all to see. I was mortified, as was David. It comes as no surprise to me that David now has a boyfriend while I have a girlfriend.

4

Gossip, Girl

I loved growing up in the South. Well, mostly. I loved the food, I loved riding around in pickup trucks with my friends, I loved the "Southern hospitality" mentality that usually came with being a part of that community. I say "usually" because while there are people in the South who are the kindest, most generous people you'll ever meet, there are also those who thrive on making as much drama as they possibly can. The primary vehicle for said drama is always gossip.

I often say that a small town's favorite sport is gossip. I realize that the entire world is obsessed with gossip, we have countless TV shows and magazines dedicated to bringing us up-to-the-minute information, whether true or fake. Still, small town gossip seems to be in a league of its own. It is a petty child's game, though more often than not, adults are its most aggressive players.

Since coming out, I've often found myself the topic of discussion with those in my hometown. I live over 2,000 miles away, but I hear the whispers nonetheless. I've heard all kinds of crazy things about myself over the past two years. Let's take a look at *My Rumors: The Greatest Hits:*

"She got engaged to her roommate." When my roommate got engaged to her boyfriend, I posted a picture of she and I holding up her newly ringed hand. The next day I got a text from my mom asking why I hadn't told her I was engaged.

"She moved over there to sin-filled Los Angeles and now she's completely letting Satan wreak havoc on her life." Cut to me sitting on my couch in Superman footie pajamas watching *Seinfeld* and eating pizza. The sheer chaos!

"She adopted a baby behind her family's back." Lesson learned, folks. Apparently, you can't post pictures of you with your friend's newborn unless you want people asking if you've secretly "lesbian adopted" a baby.

"She posts gay porn on Facebook all the time." This gem came after I shared a blog post on Facebook that was about promises I wanted to make to my future wife. Some of the promises included were things like: "I'll always take out the trash," and, "I'll watch your favorite movies." You know, your typical XXX porn stuff.

I'm not sure why people seem so shocked that I'm gay. Even before I came out, the allegations that I was "a homosexual" were no stranger to the rumor mill. I would get anonymous texts asking questions like, "u like dick or no dick?" from people who I assume were huddled around a cell phone, high-fiving each other because weren't they just the coolest? Friends made bets about my sexual orientation behind my back. An authority figure from my high school (who I didn't really get along with) called my mom to let her know that she thought I exhibited homosexual tendencies because I didn't act or dress or date like the other girls at my school. I listened from the other room as my mom angrily held back tears while defending me. She came to me afterward to ask if there was any truth to these accusations. I wanted to tell her that I wasn't sure. I wanted to tell her how confused I had been, how terrified I felt. But I couldn't. *Because what would people say?*

The funny thing is, all of these people's instincts were spot on. They were right. They could see through me even then, even when I wasn't ready to see it for myself. But even if they were right, here's the thing about a gossip: they do nothing but tear down, when they could be helping to build up. Imagine if my friends or any of the curious adults in my life had come to me and asked in earnest if I was struggling with this part of my identity. How different would my journey have looked if those people had chosen to be supportive, rather than destructive at that time in my life? How much hurt and confusion could have been avoided?

It's amazing how much power each of us has when it comes to how we make other people feel about themselves. Whether we realize it or not, we have the ability to affect and shape people, for better or for worse. I hope I never abuse my power.

5

Los Angeles Ruined My Life

I moved to Los Angeles when I was 24 years old. It was a move that made sense for me, since I have been fascinated with L.A. for as long as I can remember. I have loved movies and television and celebrities and everything else that goes into pop culture my entire life. I remember being 4 years old and riding around with my mom's best friend, Susan, running errands and listening to the radio. While on these drives, she would quiz me about celebrity couples. Who was with who? Who had broken up? Even at 4, I always knew the answers, as if I had been reading *People Magazine* for toddlers before bed every night.

For most of my life, I knew that L.A. was home to everything I loved, so why shouldn't it be home to me, too? It was hard (it's still hard) to uproot myself from everyone and everything I knew in order to live in a place where I knew no one and had no idea what would happen once I got there. Even still, I took the leap and ended up landing pretty safely. I got a good job. I made a few friends. Next up on the agenda, I needed to find a church. When I told my family and friends I was moving to L.A., most of them didn't want me to go. Not because they would miss me, or because they thought I would fail, but because they were worried about my soul. They were scared that I would move to L.A. and forget about my Christian upbringing. Most conversations I'd have with people back home at that time often revolved around one question: "Have you found a church yet?" Everyone from home was watching my every move. "Will she remain the good girl we know her to be?" I quickly found a church so that I could make church friends and remain unchanged by my new, ungodly surroundings. And I did remain unchanged. For a bit.

As you already know, I had, up to this point, been harboring feelings for girls for most of my life. Back home, these feelings were fairly easy to suppress. I was never around same sex relationships. I was surrounded by a culture where those feelings weren't accepted. I didn't have the option of exploring them. The decision was already made for me by who and what I was around. But in L.A., I started to find that everything was so much more open. I met tons of people who were gay and it became harder to ignore my own thoughts and feelings about who I was attracted to. I never had to question it before, but here, in this new place where people accepted you and allowed you to explore who you were, all I began to do was question. Am I actually gay? Do I even like church? Who am I really?

When I tried to have conversations with friends from home about the thoughts I was having, I was usually met with disgust and annoyance. "I told you L.A. was going to change you." "What are you THINKING?!" "This is just the devil confusing you!" I was now sinful to them. I wasn't the girl they knew anymore. It hurt to hear these things. It hurt that just because I had questions and was changing and growing in a direction they weren't familiar with, I was now seen as "less" in their eyes. It hurt to be told things like, "L.A. has stolen every good thing about who you are," when they weren't even bothering to listen to what I had to say.

It hurt to hear them say these things to me, but still, I was happy. For once, FINALLY, I was in a place where I could allow myself to figure out who I really am and what I really wanted. They were right, L.A. changed me, but not in the way they think.

L.A. did not strip me of my good qualities. It did not strip me of my loyalty or my sense of humor or my kindness or my generosity or my ass that won't quit. L.A. did not cause me to spin off into a life of confusion—it helped pull me out of it. This city allowed me to be around creative, loving, fun people who came alongside me to help me figure things out, people who allowed me the freedom to change and grow without judging my every step, a freedom I was not afforded back home. L.A. ruined my life, in the best way possible, and I'll never stop being thankful for it.

6

Wishy-Washy

Before I ever told any of my friends and family that I was gay, I spent a significant amount of time reading up on the biblical theology behind homosexuality and just the history of the Bible in general. You know, just some light reading for evenings and weekends. If I was going to make this life change, a change that could possibly leave me alienated from those I cared about most, I wanted to know everything there was to know about the subject. I wanted to know the history behind all of those "anti-gay" Bible verses. I wanted to know who wrote them. I wanted to know where they wrote them. I wanted to know why they wrote them. I needed to know if God really was going to smite me. I needed to know what smite even means.

Turns out, the history of the Bible and who wrote it and how we're supposed to interpret it are all very complicated, confusing things. For every scholarly article I read on who wrote these words and how I should interpret them, there were about ten others saying the exact opposite thing. "This was written by Matthew!" "No, it wasn't!" "Yes, it was!" "We think it might be, but we don't really know!" was basically all that I was learning from my trip down the theology rabbit hole. I quickly realized I wasn't going to find any 100% answers.

Still, I had the desire to handle this transition without completely disregarding my faith. I really did believe in God and I didn't feel that I needed to completely abandon my beliefs or values in order to accommodate my being gay. As far as I was concerned, being gay was who I was, it was who I had always been and if God was really who people said he was, then he had created me that way. I decided to reach out to the staff of a church in Los Angeles I had been attending for the past year. It was a pretty young church, and was much more liberal in its way of thinking than the churches I had grown up attending. Not to mention, I knew at least three other people who attended the church that were also struggling with how to handle their homosexuality in relation to their Christian beliefs. "Surely they'll be willing to talk to me and give me advice on how to go about this, especially if they know there are others in the same boat," I thought. So, I opened up my computer and sent the following email.

> Dear Pastor and/or staff,
>
> My name is Krista Doyle, and I have been attending your church for about a year now. I am writing to you because I need some advice. I have recently begun the process of preparing to tell my friends and family that I am gay, and while I don't hold the traditional view that homosexuality is sinful, I realize that most Christians do, and I'd love to talk to you or someone on your staff about how to go about

> transitioning into this life change while still staying a part of the church community.
>
> I have recently become aware of the fact that there are several people in your church struggling with this exact same thing, and I think your congregation would benefit from some type of support group, as it is scary to feel alone in this. Is there any chance of this happening?
>
> Sincerely,
> Krista

The response I received was discouraging, to say the least.

> Krista,
>
> Thanks for reaching out! Unfortunately, we do not offer these services right now. Have you tried talking to your Bible study leader? I truly believe with their prayers and words of encouragement, you'll be able to overcome these tendencies! While we do not offer small groups specifically tailored to this need, we will be starting up something called "Recovery Groups" that help people who are overcoming addiction, abuse, etc. Would you be interested in joining one of these?
>
> Alternatively, we do have short term counseling available. If you're interested in scheduling an

> appointment, please fill out the attached questionnaire so that we have a preliminary understanding of where you are in your relationship with Christ and the depth of the services you will require.
>
> In His name, Paula

THE DEPTH OF SERVICES I WILL REQUIRE? What was I, a faulty vehicle? Why would I want to join a Recovery Group? I'm not a recovering alcoholic. I wasn't going to stand up at group meetings, hold up my hand, and say things like, "Hi, my name is Krista and I'm a homosexual. It has been one day since my last homosexual thought."

It made me sad and angry that she or the church even thought homosexuality was in any way similar to addiction or abuse.

The attached questionnaire she was referring to included a series of personal questions about my faith, but I stopped reading when I got to, "Please describe in detail what it is you're seeking delivery from." Why did I have to be seeking delivery or healing? Why couldn't I just talk to them like humans and ask honest, real questions about the aspects of Christianity that I found confusing? The response crushed my naive hope that I would be able to go through this process unscathed by the church. I knew that even if I did attempt a counseling session, they would have looked over that questionnaire and immediately written me off. They would've sat me down and recycled those same 5 Bible verses that I had already been researching for months to no avail. It was then that I fully realized, *nobody had real answers.* We were all just winging it and hoping that our version of the truth was the right one.

I've since moved away quite a bit from the beliefs of modern Christianity. That may make some people in the church think that I'm a "heathen," but I know that's not true. Not much about me has changed, really. I still have the same core values. I still have the same heart. I still have the desire to have a family and raise my children to be strong, loving, good men and women. I still think that Jesus, whether a simple prophet or the son of God, had some pretty smart things to say regarding how to treat ourselves and others. And I do still believe in God. I don't know what I believe about the surrounding details, but I believe there's something up there. Or out there. Or wherever he/she/it prefers to hang around.

You may say that my new loosely held beliefs about God and Christianity make me wishy-washy, and, well, you're absolutely right. I am perhaps the wishiest-washiest believer you'll ever meet when it comes to having faith. There are times that I believe and times that I don't. Sometimes I have so many questions about who or what or why God is or isn't that it makes my head hurt. I'm okay with being wishy-washy, because the truth is, *nobody freaking knows the truth.* We can guess all we want to about the things God wants or says or does, whether he exists or whether he's just a fairy tale created to help people sleep better at night, but what arrogant assholes we would be to say that we have all the answers about such a concept. What arrogant assholes we are to personalize and chisel down beliefs until they fit the view we want to have on life, then use those beliefs as a template for how everyone else should construct their life. I guess that's the one thing we do know for certain; we can all be a bunch of arrogant assholes.

7

I Found God at The Cheesecake Factory

I met Jen about 3 months after I moved to L.A. She was also new to California and had come from Georgia, so we instantly bonded over sweet tea and Southern accents. We became fast friends and soon, we did everything together. Day drinking at the beach? All of the Fireball whiskey, please. Church every Sunday? Just like our Mamas taught us. Stalking celebrities in her Toyota Camry? Every creepy chance we got.

She put up with me when I was so obsessed with the show *Felicity* that I only wanted to drink coffee and eat cereal because *they* were only ever drinking coffee and eating cereal. Thankfully, she pulled me out of that phase before I chopped off all my hair or ran off to NYU for grad school. She happily, or at least, willingly, let me drag her along on all of my dumbest adventures, including the time I wanted to drive an hour and a half to a Wal-Mart in Riverside to find a copy of *The Bodyguard* the day Whitney Houston died because there were none left in L.A. She was a trooper. One of my favorite things we did together was eating at our favorite chain restaurants when we were feeling a little homesick. Nothing says middle America quite like Chili's, Olive Garden, Outback Steakhouse, and on one particular occasion, The Cheesecake Factory.

This was it, I had decided. I was ready to tell someone I'm gay. The week before, I had gone on a date with a guy as a last attempt at dating men, he was the "Hail Mary" pass I threw in an attempt to keep my "straight life." The pass came up short. On paper, he was perfect for me—charming, handsome, fun, liked to eat Taco Bell. But at the end of the night, he reached for my hand while I reached for the doorknob. Yep. Gay.

It was time to tell someone. That someone would be Jen. Here. At The Cheesecake Factory. I was a little nervous because Jen was a Christian. She was my church buddy, but was a great deal more conservative than I was. I knew that I was risking my very first "Hi, I'm gay" on someone who could respond very negatively. Maybe she would make me feel stupid. Maybe she would tell me we couldn't be friends anymore. Maybe she would ask the Cheesecake Factory staff for a glass of holy water so she could sprinkle the gay away. I wasn't sure what to expect, but I knew that I needed to finally tell someone the truth. I had recently come to terms with it myself and now that I was sure, keeping it inside was driving me insane. I needed someone to know who I was. Who I really was.

So here I was, mentally preparing to deliver my very first coming out speech and I could not have been more terrified. Jen and I had our differences in beliefs, yes, but she loved me, right? After all, she had been the one to console me after Whitney Houston's death! There was no breaking such a bond, at least that's what I was hoping. "Do you know what you're going to get yet?" she asked. Of course I didn't know what I wanted. Does anybody ever know what they want at Cheesecake Factory? The menu is thirty years long. I shook my head, still nervous and trying to decide when to bring up my news. "Are you okay?" she asked. Crap. I guess I actually had to do this.

Me: Jen. I need to tell you something.

Jen: Okay?

Me: You know how sometimes we joke about how we like to look at Scarlett Johansson's boobs? Or how we would probably make out with Santana from *Glee*?

Jen: Yeah…

Me: Well. I don't really think that I'm joking. I think I like girls.

Jen: Like in a gay way.

Me: Yes. Like in a gay way.

Jen: Oh. Well. Have you told anyone else?

Me: No, you're the first person. Don't worry, I'm not in love with you. You're not my type.

Jen: Rude. But okay, good.

Me: Okay.

Jen: Is there someone who is your type?

Me: Yes. It's kind of weird saying all this stuff out loud.

Jen: It's okay. I want to hear it. I'm glad you trusted me. I am curious, though, how is this going to affect your view on Christianity and God and stuff?

I nervously pushed around the food on my plate and just said, "I don't know." She let me be okay with not knowing, which meant more than she'll ever know. And that was basically it. She didn't yell at me. She didn't start reciting Bible verses or telling me the things I was feeling weren't real. She listened. She listened as I told her everything that was going on in my head. She listened as I told her about the girl I had recently developed feelings for. She helped me feel safe and, for once, at ease in my own skin. Her loving, understanding reaction helped me to feel brave enough to start coming out to the rest of my friends and family. It gave me the confidence that everything would turn out okay.

After that conversation, I felt like if there was a God, this is what having a conversation with him must be like. Honest. Encouraging. Humbling. Refreshing. I was about to tell her this when she opened her mouth, still full of cheesecake, and said, "So. ScarJo's boobs..."

8

You Never Forget Your First Inappropriate Crush

A few months before I came out, a friend of mine took me to her sister's birthday party and it kind of changed my life. "I know you're a Christian, so I don't know if this will bother you, but my sister is a lesbian and so are most of her friends," she warned. "Oh, duh, like I care." I tried to play it off like it wasn't a big deal, but I was secretly intrigued. Once we got to the party, however, I was a nervous wreck. I had been wrestling with wondering if I was a lesbian for the past few months, but I had never really been around other lesbians and now here I was, about to observe the elusive creatures in their natural habitat. How was I supposed to act? What if I accidentally flirted? I wasn't ready to flirt! Oh god, what if someone flirted with *me*? I didn't want them to, but also, I *did* want them to. I felt like my throat was closing in, but I tried to play it cool.

"Krista, this is my sister, Emily." Oh no. She looked pretty. "Hi," she said, "You can just call me Em." Oh no. She sounded pretty. I was immediately smitten. She seemed like everything I had ever been curious about wrapped up in a smoky leather jacket. I think she could sense this, because over the next several weeks we developed quite a flirty rapport. I was so drawn to her in a way that I had never experienced before. Sure, I had dated guys, but those "relationships" always felt forced and also lacked attraction, both emotional and physical. My infatuation with Emily was definitely one of the things that pushed me over the edge from "Am I gay?" to "Oh okay, so I'm like, super gay."

One of the strangest side effects of coming out was the fact that I was immediately hurled into what I like to refer to as my second puberty. I was finally allowing myself to be attracted to people I found attractive and it seemed as if my teen years were catching up to me all at once. At 24, I finally got to be 16. I finally understood what it meant to want to make out with someone until both of our faces fell off. Of course, these fresh adolescent hormones meant that my first crush was intensified x1,000—for better or for worse.

It didn't help that the situation already wasn't the best or safest for me to go diving into headfirst the way that I did. Firstly, Emily was a single mom. What on Earth did I know about taking care of kids? I slept on a mattress on the floor, had holes in all my shoes, and ate beef stew out of a can several times a week. I was lucky I could keep myself afloat, much less venture into helping someone else take care of their child. Secondly, she had major ex-girlfriend problems with not one ex, but two. They were both still very present in her life and instead of saying "See ya" and removing myself from that situation, I, in my rose-colored delusion, became even more determined to win her over.

I was what can only be described as a complete fool over the next few months, both by her doing and by my own. There were so many cringe-worthy moments that I now hate myself for:

I wrote her two songs.

At the time, I was attempting to learn the banjo and I used what few chords I knew to write two songs about her. Thankfully, she never heard them and I've blocked the lyrics from my memory.

I showed up at her place of work to declare my "love."

Yep. I pulled the ultimate stalker move. I drove 45 minutes to the hospital she worked at with the intentions of spilling my guts with a speech that I was SURE would make her mine. I got there and we literally sat in silence for 10 minutes because I was too embarrassed to speak after the realization of what I had just done slowly set in.

I went on a date with her even after she talked to her ex-girlfriend on the phone almost the whole way to the restaurant.

At one point during this mess, she asked me on a date. A real, live date. I was ecstatic! She picked me up and a few minutes later, her phone rang. It was her ex. "Don't pick up, don't pick up, don't pick up," I thought to myself. She picked up. I sat there awkwardly while she talked to her ex-girlfriend and then I STILL WENT ON THE DATE. Idiot.

I got drunk so she'd like being around me.

This is the dumbest thing about who I was at the time this was all happening. I noticed that she'd flirt more with me when we were drinking, so I drank a lot that summer. A lot. Even when I didn't want to and even when it made me feel gross. Hey, everybody? Don't do this.

I left sappy love notes around her house.

Sometimes, Emily's sister and I (who I was still close with and who HATED the situation) would stay over on the weekends and hang out. I don't remember exactly how many corny little love notes I left around her house, but they were plentiful and I'm sure they gave her and her friends and her exes a good laugh.

I ditched friends and snuck off to meet her.

None of my friends approved of my little fling with Emily. They knew it was unhealthy and wanted me to find something better for myself. So what did I do? I ignored them because "what do they know?" I lied to them a lot. I made up excuses for why I couldn't hang out so that I could go see her instead. I was a really shitty friend.

I let myself be taken advantage of. A lot.

Even at the time, I had the sneaking suspicion that Emily didn't really like me as much as she liked the attention I gave her. She had a lot of craziness going on in her life and it had to feel nice to have someone new think you are great and want to follow you around like a little puppy. Deep down, I knew this was what I was to her, but I didn't want to believe it. Or maybe

I did believe it and just didn't care. Either way, I let myself be used as someone's temporary high and I'm not proud of it.

A lot of what happened over the course of that bizarre quasi-friendship was the result of me being immature, selfish, and stubborn. I ignored all my gut instincts that were telling me this wasn't a healthy situation to be in and I paid for it. It's hard for me to say that I regret it, though. If it weren't for Emily, would I have still wanted to come out when I did? I don't know. True, I wouldn't have had to feel sad and rejected as much as I did in the moment, but I also wouldn't have had that catalyst for me figuring myself out in a huge way. I wouldn't have learned what I do and do not want out of a relationship. I wouldn't have learned how to trust myself better. I wouldn't have learned about healthy expectations and absolute deal breakers. I wouldn't have learned that no matter how many banjo songs you write, some things are just not right for you and you need to let that be okay.

9

Lesbian Bars Make Me Cry

In the spring of 2012, I had finally reached the point. Those in the LGBT community know the "point" I'm talking about. It's that moment when you've finally decided that the fear of having to go on one more awkward, chemistry-less date with a member of the opposite sex outweighs the fear of the possible negative reactions you may get from your family and friends after you've come out to them. Anyway, I had finally reached the point, which felt amazing and like a burden had been lifted and all of those wonderful things other people talk about when they talk about coming out. However, I realized that there was so much emphasis on coming out of the closet, but basically no information on how to handle what comes next. I had so many questions. How do I date? What's the best way to meet new friends in the LGBT community? Do I now have to wear flannel exclusively? Now that I had come out of the closet, I set out bright-eyed and bushy-tailed on my journey to learn how to be a lesbian. At times, the outcome of said journey looked bleak, but I powered through. Here are some things I learned along the way:

1. Ignore outside opinions and pressure.

It's hard to do, but once you remove yourself from the expectations of everyone else around you and just listen to yourself, you'll be much better off. Many of my days that year were spent freaking out because my friends all had conflicting opinions about how I should handle tough situations, new relationships, and just coming out in general. Advice from trusted friends is helpful and needed, but throw too many people into the mix and you can accidentally drown out the most important voice—your own.

2. Lesbian bars make me cry.

I don't know that I have ever not cried, or at least wanted to cry, at a lesbian bar. In case you didn't know, fellow lesbians, we can be scary creatures. I present to you, the three different cries I have cried at lesbian bars:

The "I got sneak attack kissed outside" cry.

It was 10 PM on a Friday night, so naturally, I was getting tired. I told my friends inside that I was going to head home to the safety of my bed and season three of *Friends* and was walking past the entrance line, when, out of nowhere, a girl grabs my arm, pulls me in, and starts kissing me in front of everyone. I was mortified. This may seem mild to most of you, but keep in mind that up until this point I had only kissed one other girl, one other time. And that was a person I knew and liked, not just some hyper aggressive Jane Doe!

You should also keep in mind that I am a person who holds Topher Grace's classic line, "Guard your carnal treasure," from *Win a Date with Tad Hamilton* as a personal mantra. So, there I was, in front of all these people, with Jane Doe's tongue down my throat and all I wanted to do was drop to my knees and scream, "NOT MY CARNAL TREASUUUURE!" at the top of my lungs with arms stretched to the sky.

The "My long-time crush had just rejected me and I wanted to be anywhere but a bar" cry.

The day after my very first, very intense girl crush had rejected me, a friend of mine decided that I needed to get out and meet new people, which is a totally normal way of thinking for other people who aren't me. I am basically the CW of people, so I was handling my recent rejection like a weepy adolescent from a teen drama starring Chad Michael Murray. I sat at the bar (lost in deep, important, poetic thoughts, probably), when a girl sat next to me. She started hitting on me and I immediately started crying. As if that weren't ridiculous enough, instead of running away as fast as she could, she CONTINUED TO HIT ON ME, which of course resulted in more crying. I'm laughing as I type these words, but am happy to be done with that particular episode of my teen drama.

The "Draco Malfoy won't take no for an answer" cry.

One night while we were out for a friend's birthday, we ran into a creepy Draco Malfoy look-alike who unfortunately chose me as her prey for the night. I was out on the dance floor, posted up on the wall (a little because it makes me feel cool and a lot because I dance like Elaine Benes), when here comes Draco asking me to dance. I respectfully declined, she disrespectfully ignored my response, and I spent the next half hour trying to pry her hand from mine, as she had taken it upon herself to intertwine our fingers in an attempt to get me to leave my wall of safety. I eventually escaped the dance floor with fingers intact, but don't worry, she found me later and continued her creepy efforts while also spilling an entire beer on me in front of my friends.

Needless to say, lesbian bars are not my thing.

3. I'm a disgrace to lesbianism! and other things I've been told.

One of the most discouraging experiences I had while on this journey was how hard it was to make friends. I wanted so badly to meet new people and form friendships and have support within this community to help me adjust to all these new experiences, but that was more complicated than expected. I got myself into some weird situations during my pursuit of these friendships and found out all these cool, new things about myself like:

You dress and talk like a lesbian, but don't sleep around with anyone...you're a disgrace to lesbianism.

Always great to hear! Then there was this gem...

You're not a REAL lesbian until you have your first hook up.

This was confusing to me because...what? There are people who think this way? Also, I didn't want to hook up with random girls I didn't like, I just wanted to guard my carnal treasure like Topher taught me. Oh, and I can't forget the classic confidence-builder…

You're a baby lesbian, you don't count.

Oh, okay!

Luckily, I quickly found out the people who were telling me these things weren't the norm and I did eventually find other, healthy friendships within the community that never tried to pressure me into things I wasn't ready for and didn't make me want to go crawling back into "the closet" with my tail between my legs.

4. Do you, bb.

Looking back, it feels silly to me that I used to think there was a certain way I had to dress or talk or act to be a lesbian, to be something I already was. Over the course of that journey to learning how to be a lesbian, I made and lost friendships, I got my feelings hurt, I had my heart broken, I made what feels like every mistake I could've possibly made. Most importantly, I learned that there is no "how-to" when it comes to figuring yourself out and learning what works best for you. Just do you, bb. Do you.

10

My Evil Gay Agenda

Something I'll never understand is what people mean when they talk about the "gay agenda." Every time I hear this phrase, it's being used to explain how the gay community are using said agenda to destroy all that is held to be good and true in our society, or how the gays are destroying our American families. What? WHAT? Are there gay town council meetings being held in the gay town hall where we discuss what to add to our evil gay agenda? Are there gay committees in charge of finding fun, new, creative gay ways to screw up our country? Is there a gay agenda leader sitting on his or her mighty throne, head thrown back in evil laughter, screaming, "Soooooon they'll alllll be gayyy!" Because that is what comes to my mind when I hear people mention the "evil gay agenda." To clear some things up, I've decided to give you a sneak peek at my own, personal gay agenda. That's right, folks–a genuine, authentic gay agenda! Here's what I, a gay, expects out of a typical day.

8 AM – Wake up. Almost.

8:30 AM – Wake up again. This time for real.

9:00 AM – Leave my house for work.

9:10 AM – Try to find something to listen to on Spotify. Ke$ha? No. Elton John? No. I settle on Nicki Minaj.

9:45 AM – Do I want McDonald's? Ugh, I do, but also, calories and grease and sugar. But who cares, I'll go. No, I shouldn't.

9:55 AM – Finish my sausage biscuit and hash brown in the parking lot at work.

10:00 AM – Go into work. Go see if they have any diet Dr. Pepper in the kitchen. They do. Do a tiny fist pump.

11:30 AM – Talk to 1 to 4 co-workers about how Hanson is still relevant.

1:00 PM – Get a burger from the food truck downstairs. They forgot the mustard, but that's okay.

1:30 PM – Hang out with the guys while I eat lunch. Watch an episode of *Workaholics* on Amazon Prime.

3:45 PM – Explain to Dan in accounting what "Surfbort" means.

7:00 PM – Leave work. This time I do pick Elton John on Spotify.

7:30 PM – Get home to my girlfriend. We talk about what we want for dinner. We want Taco Bell, but decide we can't eat that two nights in a row because, health.

8:00 PM – Girlfriend puts some sort of Trader Joe's health pizza in the oven and we both sit on the couch. We talk a little, but mostly just ignore each other and check Twitter and/or Instagram.

8:45 PM – We try to decide what to watch while we eat our pizza. She refuses to watch *Unsolved Mysteries* even though I tell her it's the complete collection of UFO episodes.

8:55 PM – We settle on *Roseanne.*

11:30 PM – We are still watching *Roseanne.*

12:00 AM – Shower. Go to sleep.

And there you have it, ladies and gents. That is a typical day in my grand plan to destroy our society and your families! The truth is, I don't understand why me being gay comes with the idea that I have malicious intent toward your beliefs and values. The gay community does not wish to destroy your families with an "evil gay agenda." To be honest, the "traditional American family" doesn't really need any help with destroying itself days. Selfishness is destroying your families. Addiction is destroying your families. Infidelity is destroying your families. Abuse is destroying your families. Me wanting to come home at night to watch Netflix with a woman instead of a man is not destroying your families. I hope that the next time you wonder what I'm thinking regarding your beliefs and values, you'll remember that I'm not.

11

For My Family

As I've been writing these stories about navigating through the weirdness and scariness and confusion of life, I've been reminded of a separate journey that has been taking place along the way: the one I have been on with my family. It hasn't been an easy one (I wasn't sure if we were going to survive my teen years), but it has been ours all the same. Nothing will ever be able to take away from what we have experienced together. They watched me learn to walk and talk and dance in my diaper. They watched me fail at Jr. High basketball and succeed at memorizing every single episode of *Friends*. They stuck by me through skinned knees and obnoxious jokes and bad decisions and more bad decisions. They watched me as I learned to drive and then again as I wrecked their car on a rogue trip to McDonald's. Most importantly, they introduced me to reading, writing, and the greatness of Whitney Houston.

I wasn't sure how they were going to react when I decided to tell them I was gay. It didn't come easy to me, to tell them news that I knew may hurt them and disappoint them and alter the way they thought of me, but I could no longer take the feeling of my family not knowing who I really was.

There were those who supported me from the get-go. When I told them, my confession was met with responses like

"Finally" and "This has been a long time coming." They told me they loved me and wanted me to be happy, no matter what. Their kind words were the encouragement and reassurance I needed to feel like everything was going to be okay.

There were those who took the news a little harder. I expected this, as I was basically telling them that I was going against things that they taught me to believe, things that they themselves had been taught to believe for the past 40+ years. There were tears shed and prayers prayed. There were angry phone calls and desperate text messages, begging me to "change my mind." I didn't expect their point of view to change overnight. After all, mine hadn't. It had taken me years of struggling my way through question after question in order to get to a point where I felt comfortable with accepting this about myself. If it had taken even me a while to come around, why should I demand that they immediately accept this huge life change they weren't expecting? Even though they felt hurt and angry, they were never cruel to me. They never threatened to stop loving me or including me in their lives. I knew that I just needed to give them time to do their own questioning and growing.

Even though things were rough at the time, I still had never felt closer to them. I never realized how much of a wall had been built between us by me hiding important parts of myself until I felt it instantly start breaking down when I came out to them. Over the past two years, I've watched them become more and more comfortable with me being a lesbian. Texts that once begged me to change my mind are now telling me that I am loved and accepted no matter what. Texts that were once page after page of Bible verses telling me I'm wrong are now texts asking to hear more about my side of things. The car which held the memory of fighting with them one Christmas Eve about being attracted to women is now the car that holds the memory of laughing with them on the way to Cracker Barrel the first time I brought my girlfriend home to meet them.

When I think about these things, I am so thankful to have family members who accept me fully, even if it took them a while to come around. I don't mind that I had to be patient in order for them to be okay with this, because I know so many others who wouldn't dare to even think of seeing such issues from any perspective other than their own. My family chose to get out of their comfort zone in order to meet me in the middle, what more could I have asked for? I often wonder what would have happened if I had met their hurt and anger with more hurt and anger. If I had shut them out due to their initial disapproval, would we be as close as we are now? Would they have been as willing to try and see the situation from my side? Would I feel as confident and healthy as I do right now? I don't know.

"Don't fight hate with hate" is a phrase we hear a lot these days, and I wish it was something that was actually put into practice more than it has been. We are so quick to anger and to lash out, and at times, that may be justified. But other times, by lashing out we are just making things worse. Someone takes a strike at us and we strike right back. We are responding to each other with hate, which stirs up more hate. We forget to have patience with other people, to react with kindness, to allow them the time to come around and meet us in the middle.

With that said, I know that not everyone comes out to a situation like mine. Not everyone has the luxury of just "waiting it out" until their loved ones decide to come around. In those cases, responding with patience and kindness may get you nowhere. In those cases, the hate may never stop. In those cases, tell those people to kiss your ass. There is a difference between being patient with someone who is attempting to adjust to your news in a healthy way and letting yourself be continuously belittled by someone who has no intention of trying to be empathetic or of trying to see your side. There is no reason you need to put up with some homophobic douchebag who refuses to stop being a douchebag just because their great-great-great-great-grandpa told them they needed to be a douchebag. Coming out is a big deal and the process leading up to it, as well as the process that follows it, can be very confusing and exciting and scary and horrible and amazing. Seek out relationships that will support you in this; there is no room for douchebags, though they make for good stories.

12

Possible Lessons to Be Learned From This Book

1. Don't write songs about your inappropriate crush on a banjo. Or the piano. You are not an Avett Brother nor are you Adele.

2. I reference TV shows too much, probably.

3. Have all emotionally intense conversations at The Cheesecake Factory.

4. Jesus is not Santa Claus.

5. It is always okay for you to ask questions about things that confuse you in life.

6. If you're going to break up with someone, do it at McDonald's using chicken nugget analogies.

7. Are you thinking about spreading a rumor about me or anyone else? If so…stop, take a deep breath, and go get an actual hobby. Perhaps knitting?

8. It is safe, but probably illegal, to carry a deceased alligator in the back seat of your car.

9. Those of us in the LGBT community do not care enough about what you do or do not believe to try and sabotage that.

10. Don't be a dick.

Acknowledgements

Hooray, I wrote a book! And you read my book! Or at least you are here, reading the acknowledgements, so for that, you are the first person I'd like to thank!

I'd also like to thank:

Thought Catalog and my editor, Mink Choi, for giving me the opportunity to tell my stories and for being patient because rewrites.

Desiree, for reading pages and re-reading pages and giving me the best advice always.

My family, for reading this even though I probably use more curse words than you'd have liked me to. Also, I promise I no longer drink as much as I did in some of these stories.

My girlfriend, Taylor, for encouraging me no matter how stressed out I got, for supporting me no matter how annoying I got. I love you. OK.

Nicki Minaj, for writing the song "I'm The Best," without which I would never have finished this book.

The Melt, for all their free Wi-Fi, also without which I would never have finished this book.

About the Author

Krista Doyle is a writer and quasi-adult who now resides in Los Angeles after spending her formative years in the cow pastures of Louisiana. She has contributed her writing to websites such as *Thought Catalog, HelloGiggles, The Conversation,* and *The Siren* and works for a really fun TV show where she gets free snacks, has an office hamster, and is a founding member of the office rollerskating club. In her free time, you can probably find her on her couch watching *Friends* or at any local Chili's drinking all of the strawberry margaritas.

Thought Catalog, it's a website.

www.thoughtcatalog.com

Social

facebook.com/thoughtcatalog
twitter.com/thoughtcatalog
tumblr.com/thoughtcatalog
instagram.com/thoughtcatalog

Corporate

www.thought.is